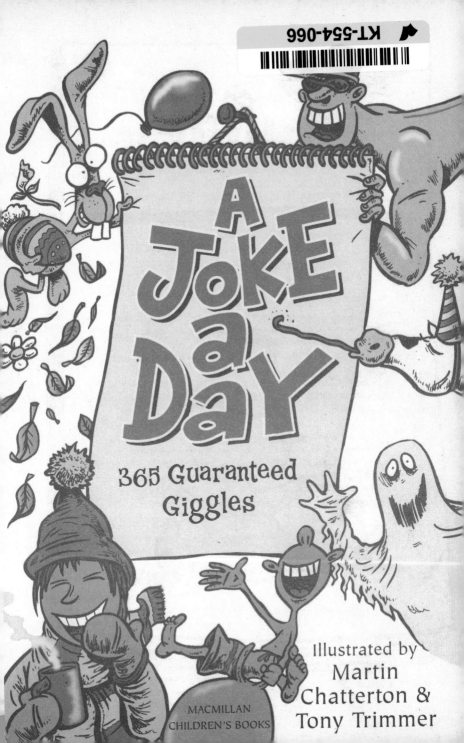

A JOKE a DaY

365 Guaranteed Giggles

Illustrated by
**Martin Chatterton &
Tony Trimmer**

MACMILLAN
CHILDREN'S BOOKS

January

January 1

New Year's Day

What's a cow's favourite holiday?
Moo Year's Day!

January 2

Why do bees hum?
Because they don't know the words.

January 3

What do you get if you cross a skunk with a dinosaur?
A stinkasaurus.

January 4

Customer: Excuse me, waiter, is there spaghetti on the menu?
Waiter: No, madam, I wiped it off.

January 5

What's a polygon?
A dead parrot.

January 6

Epiphany

Who works in a department store selling perfume?
Frank Incense.

  Why do cows
have bells?
*Because their
horns don't work.*

 What did the mummy
say to the detective?
"Let's wrap this case up."

What's yellow,
brown, and hairy?
*Cheese on toast
dropped on the carpet.*

Why is it difficult to hold a conversation with a goat?
It always butts in.

What smells, runs all day, and lies around at night with its tongue hanging out?
A pair of old trainers.

Why did the chicken
cross the clothes shop?
To get to the other size.

"You're late," said
one frog to the other.
"I know," he replied.
"I got stuck in
someone's throat."

What kind of
bird can write?
A pen-guin.

January 15

What do dogs call parking meters?
Pay toilets!

January 16

What goes trot-dash-trot-dash-dash?
Horse code.

January 17

What do you get when you cross a cat with a vacuum cleaner?
I don't know but it drinks a lot of milk!

What did the horse say when he reached the end of his nosebag?
"That's the last straw."

What do you call a fairy that hasn't washed?
Stinkerbell.

What do you get if you walk under a cow?
A pat on the head.

Squirrel Appreciation Day

How can you catch a squirrel?
Climb up a tree and act like a nut.

A duck went into a chemist's and asked for some ointment. "Certainly," said the chemist. "Shall I put it on your bill?"

What did the mother buffalo say to her son before he left?
"Bison."

January
24

What's worse than taking a bite of your apple and seeing a worm?
Seeing half a worm.

January
25

What do you get from a well-educated oyster?
Pearls of wisdom.

January
26

Australia Day

What do you call a lazy kangaroo?
A pouch potato.

Thomas Crapper Day

What vegetable can you find in a toilet?

A leek.

How can you tell if an elephant is getting ready to charge?

He pulls out his credit card.

What do you get if you put a young goat in a blender?

A crazy, mixed-up kid.

What does a bat
sing in the rain?
*"Raindrops keep
falling on my feet."*

What did the first
cannibal say to the
second cannibal
after they had
eaten a clown?
*"Is it me or did that
taste a little bit funny?"*

February

Why did the boy go to bed early?
Because he was feeling Febru-weary.

Groundhog Day

What happened when the groundhog met the dog catcher?
It became a pound hog!

What do you call a fly with no wings?
A walk.

What fairytale do ghosts like best?
Sleeping boo-ty.

Why does Batman wear his underwear outside of his trousers?
To keep them clean.

What do you give a seasick elephant?
Lots of room.

February 7

What did the biker have written on his leather jacket?
If you can read this, my girlfriend has fallen off!

February 8

Kite Flying Day

"Doctor, doctor, I've got so much wind. Do you have anything for it?"
"Yes, here's a kite. Now go and fly it."

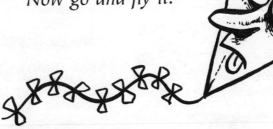

Why do seagulls
live by the sea?
*Because if they lived
in the bay, they'd be
called bagels.*

What do you call a frog
with no hind legs?
Unhoppy!

How can you double
your money?
By folding it in half.

Johnny: Dad, today is Lincoln's Birthday. He was a great man, wasn't he?

Dad, always eager to teach his young son a lesson: Yes, Johnny, indeed he was. And mind you, when Abraham Lincoln was your age, he was out splitting rails.

Johnny: Yes, Dad, I know. And when he was your age, he was President of the United States.

What's red, sweet and bites people?
A jampire.

What happens when you fall in love with a chef?
You get buttered up.

What's a dirty book?
One that's been dropped in the toilet.

Why do witches fly on broomsticks?
Vacuum cleaner cords aren't long enough.

What do you get if you cross a turkey with a banjo?

A bird that plucks itself.

Teacher: Give me three collective nouns.

Pupil: Wastepaper basket, vacuum cleaner, and a dustpan.

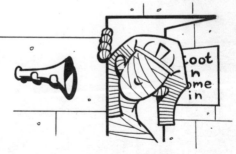

What did it say on the door of the pharaoh's tomb?

Toot 'n' come in.

What do you get if you cross a dog with a telephone?
A golden receiver.

What's grey, has big ears and a trunk?
A mouse going on holiday.

Where did George Washington buy his hatchet?
At the chopping mall.

Where can elephants be found?
Don't be silly, they're much too big to lose.

Why did the hedgehog cross the road?
To show that he had guts.

What do you get if you drop a piano down a mine shaft?
A flat minor.

What stands in the middle of Paris?
The letter "r".

What kind of streets do zombies like best?
Dead ends.

Why do doctors and nurses wear masks?
So if they make a mistake, the patient won't know who did it!

(Leap years only)

What years do frogs like best?
Leap years.

March

Pig Day

What do you call a pig that does karate?
Pork chop.

What books do owls read?
Hoot-dunits.

What kind of tree is good at maths?
A geometry.

What is black and white and red all over?
A nun in a blender.

Why did the dinosaur cross the road?
Because the chicken hadn't been invented yet.

Dentist's Day

What did the dentist of the year get?
A little plaque.

Why did the boy bring toilet paper to the party?
Because he's a party pooper.

Why do birds fly south in winter?
Because it's too far to walk.

What do you call a man with no legs?
Neil.

What farm animal talks too much?
Blah Blah Black Sheep.

How can you tell which spiders are the trendiest?
They have their own websites.

Why did the boy take his car to school?
To drive his teacher up the wall.

March
13

Which bird is
always out of
breath?
A puffin.

March
14

What goes "quick, quick"?
A duck with hiccups.

March
15

What happened when
the witch was naughty
at school?
She was ex-spelled.

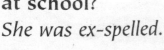

What's the most important thing to remember in a chemistry lesson?
Don't lick the spoon.

St Patrick's Day

What is Irish and on the lawn all summer?
Paddy O'Furniture.

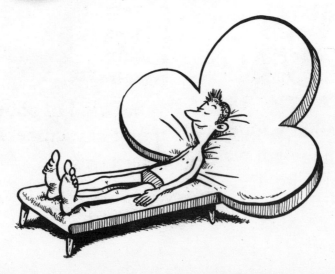

March 18

What do you call a cow with no feet? *Ground beef.*

March 19

What's big and grey and has body odour problems? *A smellyphant.*

March 20

What kind of ghosts haunt skyscrapers? *High spirits.*

What happened to the two bedbugs who fell in love?
They got married in the spring.

International Goof-off Day

Teacher: Gavin, don't hum while you're working.
Gavin: I'm not working, miss, just humming.

Why is a bunny the luckiest animal in the world?
It has four rabbit's feet.

How do hedgehogs play leapfrog?
Very carefully.

Who invented fractions?
Henry the Eighth.

Why were the naughty eggs punished?
Because they kept playing practical yolks.

What do you get if you cross the Atlantic with the *Titanic*?
Halfway.

What happened to the boy who drank eight cans of coke?
He brought 7-Up.

What do you call a lost monster?

A where-wolf.

Doctor's Day

"Doctor, Doctor, I feel like a pack of cards."

"I'll deal with you later."

Why shouldn't you tell an egg a good joke?

It might crack up.

April

April
1

April Fool's Day

Why is everyone tired on April first?
They've just finished a 31 day March!

April
2

When do monkeys fall from the sky?
During Ape-ril showers.

Why do polar bears have fur coats?
They don't look good in tweed ones.

What do you get if you pour hot water down a rabbit hole?
Hot cross buns.

Why did the teacher turn on the lights?
Because her pupils were so dim.

$$1 + 1 = 11$$

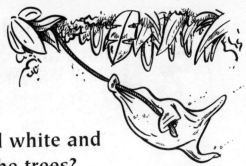

What's green and white and
swings through the trees?
Tarzan's hankie!

What do you get if you cross
an elephant with a sparrow?
Broken telephone wires.

What kind of jewellery
do rabbits wear?
14 carrot gold.

April
9

"Mummy, mummy, all the kids call me a werewolf!"
"Never mind, dear, now go and comb your face."

April
10

Teacher: If you had five chocolate bars and your little brother asked you for one, how many would you have left?
Pupil: Five, of course.

April
11

What happened when the dog went to the flea circus?
He stole the show.

How do chickens
stay in shape?
They eggsercise.

What do you call
bears with no ears?
B.

What do you call a
fish with no eyes?
A fsh.

Teacher: Can anyone tell me the name of the Dog Star?

Pupil: Lassie?

How do witches keep their hair in place while flying?

With scare spray.

What's brown and sounds like a bell?

Dung.

April 18

Why did the boy take a ladder to school?
Because it was a high school.

April 19

What season is it when you are on a trampoline?
Spring.

April
20

How many rotten eggs were in the omelette?
A phew.

April
21

Where did the vampire keep his valuables?
In a blood bank.

April
22

Earth Day

How can you tell if a tree is a Dogwood?
By its bark!

April
23

What do you call a
naughty monkey?
A bad-boon.

April
24

Why was the
bunny so upset?
*He was having a
bad hare day.*

April
25

What do you call a boomerang that won't come back?
A stick.

April
26

Why was the boy sitting in the gerbils' cage?
Because he wanted to be the teacher's pet.

April
27

What tools are used in arithmetic?
Multipliers.

April 28

What is a skeleton's favourite musical instrument?

A trombone.

April 29

INTERNATIONAL DANCE DAY

Why are dogs such bad dancers?

They have two left feet.

April 30

What's the worst thing you'll find in the school canteen?

The food.

May

Why do rhinos have so many wrinkles?
Because they are hard to iron.

Why did the cell cross the microscope?
To get to the other slide.

Why did the demon undertaker chop up corpses?
He wanted them to rest in pieces.

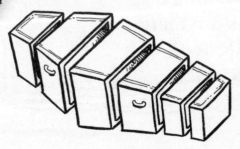

Respect for Chickens Day

What do you call a chicken who crosses the road, rolls around in mud and then comes back?
A dirty double-crosser.

Cinco de Mayo

What kind of cans are there in Mexico?
Mexicans!

Teacher: How do you like doing your homework?
Pupil: I like doing nothing better!

What do you get if you cross an elephant and a parakeet?
A very messy cage.

What game do cannibals play?
Swallow the leader.

What's worse than a giraffe with a sore throat?
A centipede with verrucas.

What do dogs increase?
The pup-ulation.

What did the daddy ghost say to his family when driving?
"Fasten your sheet belts."

May 12

What should you do if you give an elephant chilli?
Get out of the way.

May 13

What's green with red spots?
A frog with chickenpox.

May 14

What do you put on a pig's pimple?
Oinkment.

May 15

What do they teach at witch school?
Spelling.

May 16

Why aren't leopards good at playing hide and seek?
They're always spotted.

May 17

Why did knights in armour practise a lot?
To stop them from getting rusty.

May 18

How do ghosts like their eggs cooked?
Terrifried!

MAY
19

What's a vampire's favourite dance?
The fangdango.

MAY
20

What do you call the small rivers that run into the Nile?
Juveniles.

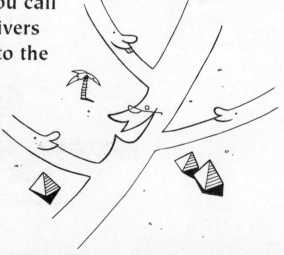

Why did the hedgehog squeal "Ouch, ouch, ouch!"?
Because he put his coat on inside out.

What goes cluck, cluck . . . BANG?
A chicken in a minefield.

May
23

world Turtle Day

What did the snail say when he rode on the turtle's back?
"Wheeee!"

May
24

Why don't mummies go on holiday?
They're afraid they'll relax and unwind.

What kind of food do maths teachers eat?
Square meals.

What's the hardest thing about learning to ride a horse?
The ground.

How do you keep a monster from biting his nails?
Give him some screws.

May 28

whale Day

What do you call a whale band?

An orca-stra.

May 29

Mother: Eat your greens, they're good for your skin.

Boy: But I don't want green skin!

Yuck!

May 30

What happened to the glow-worm when he was squashed?
He was de-lighted.

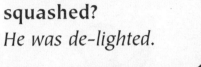

May 31

What do you call a monster with no neck?
The Lost Neck Monster.

JuNe

JUNE

1

How do you get rid
of termites?
Ex-terminite them.

JUNE

2

What do lions call antelopes?
Fast food.

JUNE

3

**What do you call
a sleeping bull?**
A bulldozer.

Why are cavemen similar to teenagers?
They like to go clubbing.

"Mummy, mummy, the other kids keep calling me a bighead."
"Don't worry, darling, there's nothing in it."

Do you want to hear the joke about the pencil?
No. It's pointless.

What do you get if you cross a rabbit with shallots?
Bunnions.

What day do fish hate?
Fry day.

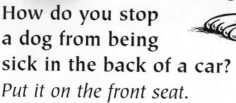

How do you stop
a dog from being
sick in the back of a car?
Put it on the front seat.

What do you get if
you cross a dinosaur
with a wizard?
Tyrannosaurus Hex.

How do you make a milkshake?
Sneak up behind a glass of milk and yell "Boo!"

Why doesn't anyone like Dracula?
He has a bat temper.

Why don't hippos ride bicycles?
The helmets don't fit them.

June **14**

What do American monkeys wave on Flag Day?
Star Spangled Bananas!

June **15**

What game do cows play at parties?
Moosical chairs.

JUNE 16

Why were Ancient Egyptian children confused?
Because their daddies were mummies.

JUNE 17

world Juggling Day

How do you kill a circus?
You go for the juggler.

Have you heard about the good-weather witch?
She's forecasting sunny spells.

June **19**

Butterfly Day

Why couldn't the butterfly go to the dance?
It was a moth ball.

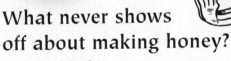

What never shows
off about making honey?
A humble bee.

Who was the most
famous French skeleton?
Napoleon Bone-apart.

What do you get
when you run
over a parakeet
with a lawn
mower?
Shredded tweet.

Who lost a herd of elephants?
Big Bo Peep.

What's the difference between a toilet brush and a biscuit?
You can't dip a toilet brush in your tea.

June 25

What goes, "Ha, ha, ha – thud"?
A monster laughing his head off.

June 26

Why are giraffes so slow to apologize?
It takes them a long time to swallow their pride.

What do demons have for breakfast?
Devilled eggs.

What's the difference between an Indian elephant and an African elephant?
About 3000 miles.

June 29

What's the best thing about school?

Holidays.

BBBRRiiiNNG!!

June 30

What's a crocodile's favourite card game?

Snap.

July

Canada Day

What did the beaver say to the tree?

"It's been nice gnawing you."

What is a vampire's favourite ice cream flavour?

Veinilla.

Father: Didn't you hear me call you?

Son: Yes, but you told me not to answer back.

What do you call an American dog?

A Yankee Poodle.

July
5

What do you call a dirty Teletubby?

Stinky-winky.

What do you call a
cat eating a lemon?
Sour puss.

What does the queen
do if she burps?
She issues a royal pardon.

Why did the lion
lose at poker?
*Because he was playing
with a cheetah.*

July 9

How do you identify
a bald eagle?
*All his feathers are
combed over to one side.*

July 10

What did the teddy bear say
when he was offered dessert?
"No thanks, I'm stuffed."

July
11

What do you get if you cross a dog with a skunk?
Rid of the dog.

July
12

Who exploded at Waterloo?
Napoleon Blownapart.

July
13

What ride do spirits like best at the amusement park?
The rollerghoster.

Why can't executioners learn French?
Because they know no merci.

Where do cows go on holiday?
Moo York.

What is Dracula's favourite fruit?
A neck-tarine.

How do you get milk from a cat?
Steal her saucer.

What do you get if you cross a dog and a frog?
A croaker spaniel.

What kind of fish do you find in a birdcage?
A perch.

Why was the stable
boy so busy?
*Because his work
kept piling up.*

July
21

How do you make a
witch scratch?
Just take away the "w".

July
22

Why can't you hear a
pterodactyl go to the toilet?
Because it has a silent "p".

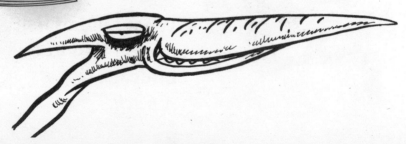

July 23

Boy: I thought we had a choice for dinner but there's only salad.
Mother: *That's the choice – take it or leave it!*

July 24

If you were in the mid-Atlantic facing south, what would be on your right hand?
Four fingers and a thumb.

July 25

Why can't skeletons play music in church?
Because they have no organs.

Did you hear about the stupid dog that laid down to eat a bone? *When he stood up, he only had three legs.*

How many insects are needed to fill an apartment block? *Tenants.*

Hamburger Day

Why did the hamburger go to the gym? *To get better buns.*

How do sheep celebrate their birthdays?
By singing Happy Birthday to Ewe!

What do you call a dead cow that's come back to life?
Zombeef.

 Why did the cannibal join the police force?
So he could grill his suspects.

August

August 1

How can you tell the difference between tinned beans and tinned custard?
Read the labels.

August 2

What happened to the dog who ate garlic?
His bark was worse than his bite.

August 3

"Doctor, doctor, do the tests show that I'm normal?"
"Yes, yes, both your heads are fine."

What has antlers and sucks blood?
A moose-quito.

What's the difference between a brussels sprout and a bogey?
You can't get a kid to eat a brussels sprout.

Where can you buy a chess set?
At a pawn shop.

August 7

What kind of bears like bad weather?
Drizzly bears.

August 8

What type of music does a ghost like?
Anything he can boo-gie to.

August 9

What happened to the shark who swallowed a bunch of keys?
He got lockjaw.

August 10

Why didn't the angry witch ride her broom?
She was afraid of flying off the handle.

August 11

What's so great about a neurotic doll?

It comes already wound up.

August 12

Elvis Presley Commemoration Day

What is green and sings?

Elvis Parsley.

August 13

What do you get if you eat baked beans and onions?

Tear gas.

What do you get if you cross a toad with a galaxy?
Star warts.

Why did the vampire subscribe to *The Wall Street Journal*?
He heard it had a great circulation.

What's the best thing to put into a roast dinner?
Your teeth!

August 17

Sandcastle Day

What do you call
a witch who lives
at the beach?
A sand-witch.

August 18

"Waiter, waiter,
there's a hand in
my soup?"
*"That's not your
soup, sir, that's a
finger bowl."*

What happens when two snails have a fight?
They slug it out.

What did the Japanese tourist wear in Alaska?
An Eskimono.

What happened to the guy who didn't pay his exorcist?

He was repossessed.

Be An Angel Day

What did one angel say to the other angel?

"Halo there!"

Why did the flea lose his job?
It wasn't up to scratch.

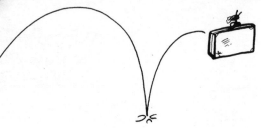

Mother: I know you're disappointed with your birthday present, Billy, but remember – it's the thought that counts.
Billy: Couldn't you have thought a little bigger?

August 25

What's a monster's favourite bean?
A human bean.

August 26

Toilet Paper Day

Why did the toilet paper roll down the hill?
It wanted to get to the bottom.

August 27

What's black and white and eats like a horse?
A zebra.

August 28

What do you give a sick snake?
Asp-irin.

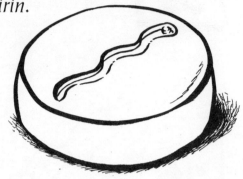

August 29

What's the best time to buy budgies?
When they're going cheep.

August
30

What does a skeleton order at a restaurant?
Spare ribs.

August
31

What did the judge say to the skunk?
"Odour in the courtroom!"

September

What's grey and goes round and round?
An elephant in a washing machine.

What do ghosts have for dessert?
Boo-berry ice scream.

What did the frog say at the dinner party?
"Time's fun when you're having flies."

What do you call a stupid skeleton?
Bonehead.

Teacher: Why are you always late for school?
Pupil: Because you keep ringing the bell before I get here.

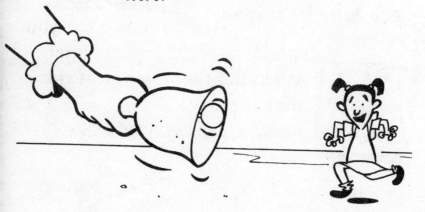

September 6

Why was the head teacher worried?
Because there were so many rulers in the school.

September 7

Why are fish so clever?
They live in schools.

September 8

Teacher: I hope I didn't see you looking at Fred's exam paper.
Pupil: I hope you didn't either.

September
9

Why do dogs run in circles?
It's hard to run in pentagons.

September
10

Teacher: Can anyone name a liquid that won't freeze?
Pupil: Hot water?

September 11

Why did the teacher wear sunglasses?
Because her pupils were so bright.

September 12

What has four wheels, gives milk and eats grass?
A cow on a skateboard.

September 13

International Chocolate Day

What did the boy say to his chocolate bar?
"Nice to melt you."

September 14

What do snakes like to study at school?

Hissssstory.

September 15

What do you call two people who embarrass you at Parents' Evening?

Mum and Dad.

No!

September
16

Tunday
Tonday
Triday
Tednesday

Teacher: Name two days of the week that begin with "t".
Pupil: Today and tomorrow.

September
17

What's the difference between school dinners and dog food?
School dinners come on plates.

September
18

What kind of jewellery do witches wear?
Charm bracelets.

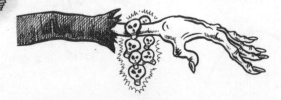

September
19

<u>Talk Like a Pirate Day</u>

What did one pirate say to the other?

"How AAARRRGGGGHHHHH you doing?"

September
20

Why don't skeletons ever go out on the town?

Because they don't have any body to go out with.

How do you know it is raining cats and dogs?
You step in a poodle.

Teacher: Write the longest sentence you can.
Pupil: Easy! "Life imprisonment".

Why did the secretary have all her fingers chopped off?
Because she wanted to do shorthand.

Punctuation Day

How can you tell a cat from a comma?
A cat has claws at the end of its paws, and a comma's a pause at the end of a clause.

September

25

Why do giraffes have long necks?
Because their feet smell.

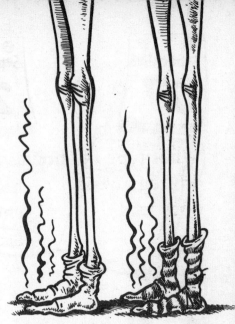

September

26

What is a vampire's favourite sport?
Casketball.

September 27

What type of shoes do frogs wear?
Open toad.

September 28

What is Beethoven doing in his grave?
Decomposing.

What do you do when a pig has a heart attack?
Call a hambulance!

<u>Pumpkin Day</u>

What is a pumpkin's favourite sport?
Squash.

October

October

1

What is a baby ghost's favourite game?

Peeka-BOO!

October

2

Why didn't the skeleton cross the road?

He didn't have the guts.

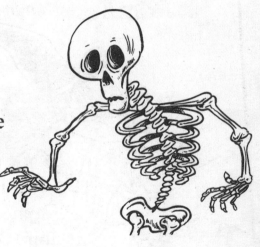

October

3

What type of dog do vampires like the best?

Bloodhounds.

October
4

Why do mummies have trouble keeping friends?
They're too wrapped up in themselves.

October
5

What do you call someone who keeps on talking even when no one is listening?
A teacher.

October
6

What's big and green and goes, "Oink, oink"?
Frankenswine.

October
7

Why was the witch kicked out of school?
Because she failed spelling.

October
8

Who was the famous skeleton detective?
Sherlock Bones.

October
9

Why wasn't the vampire working?
He was taking a coffin break.

October 10

What happened to the wolf who fell into the washing machine?
He became a wash-and-werewolf.

October 11

What is a mummy's favourite type of music?
Wrap!

October 12

Why did the one-eyed monster have to close his school?
He only had one pupil.

October 13

What kind of pets do ghosts have?
Scaredy cats.

October 14

Why does Dracula take art classes?
He likes to draw blood.

Why are skeletons so calm?
Nothing gets under their skin.

What kind of piano music do witches play?
Hag-time.

Why do vampires need mouthwash?
They have bat breath.

October
18

**Why are pixies such
messy eaters?**
*Because they are always
goblin their food.*

October
19

**Why did the headless
horseman go into business?**
He wanted to get ahead in life.

October
20

**What do you
call a wizard
from outer
space?**
A flying sorcerer.

How do monsters predict the future?
They read their horrorscope.

Why isn't Dracula invited to many parties?
He's a pain in the neck.

Where do ghosts go swimming?
The Dead Sea.

What do you call two witches who live together?
Broommates.

What trees do ghouls like best?
Ceme-trees!

What do you call a prehistoric ghost?
A terror-dactyl.

October
27

Why did the vampire go to the orthodontist?
To improve his bite.

October
28

Why did the ghost starch her sheet?
So she could scare everyone stiff.

October
29

What do skeletons say before eating?
"Bone Appetit!"

October 30

What do you get if you cross a witch with an iceberg?
Cold spells.

October 31

Halloween

What do you do when fifty zombies surround your house?
Hope it's Halloween!

November

November
1

What did the slug say as he fell off a branch?
"How slime flies."

November
2

All Soul's Day

What kind of music do ghosts like?
Spirituals.

November
3

Man: Can I have a parrot for my son, please?
Pet Shop Owner: Sorry, sir, we don't do swaps here.

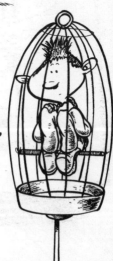

November 4

What did the donkey who only had weeds to eat say?

"Thistle have to do."

November 5

Guy Fawkes Night (UK)

What do you get when you cross a dinosaur with fireworks?

Dinomite.

November 6

Why did Dracula visit the doctor?
Because of his coffin.

November 7

Why did the owl say "Tweet, tweet"?
Because she didn't give a hoot.

Boy snake: Dad, are we poisonous?
Dad snake: Yes, son, why do you ask?
Boy snake: I've just bitten my tongue.

What do you get when you cross a penguin and an alligator?
I don't know, but don't try to fix its bow tie.

Why did the fly fly?
Because the spider spied her.

Why is it difficult to keep a secret when you're cold?
Because your teeth chatter.

What do you call a sheep with no legs or head?
A cloud.

What does a short-sighted gingerbread man use for eyes?
Contact raisins.

Why can't two elephants go swimming at the same time?
They only have one pair of trunks.

What do you call a chicken in a shell suit?
An egg.

What do you give a sick canary?
Tweetment.

Why did the skeleton stay up late studying?
He was boning up for his exams.

November 18

What did the bald man say when he got a comb for his birthday?

"Thanks, I'll never part with it."

November 19

How can you identify a maths plant?

It has square roots.

November 20

Where's the best place to have the school nurse's office?
Next to the cafeteria.

November 21

What was the cold, evil candle called?
The wicked wick of the north.

November
22

Why won't banks allow kangaroos to open accounts?
Their cheques always bounce.

November
23

What bird has wings but cannot fly?
Roast chicken.

November
24

What do you call a sick dog?
A Germy Shepherd.

November 25

What do vampires put
on their dinner?
Grave-y.

November 26

"Waiter, waiter, there's a
fly in my soup!"
*"Well, throw it a pea and it
can play water polo."*

November 27

Why did they let the turkey join the band?

Because it had drumsticks.

November 28

Where do ponies go when they're ill?

The horse-pital.

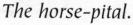

November
29

What did the frog order at the fast-food restaurant?
French flies and a diet croak.

November
30

Teacher: Who can tell me what the Scots mean by "lads and lasses"?
Pupil: I know! Lads are boys and lassies are dogs.

December

What do you have in December that you don't have in any other month?
The letter "d".

How does Rudolf know when Christmas is coming?
He looks at his calen-deer.

What is green, covered with tinsel and says, "Ribbet, ribbet"?
A mistle-toad.

December
4

Who brings
Christmas presents
to baby sharks?
Santa Jaws.

December
5

How do Chihuahuas
say Merry Christmas?
Fleas Navidog!

December
6

Why do mummies
like Christmas so
much?
*Because of all the
wrapping!*

December 7

What's red, white and blue at Christmas-time?
A sad candy cane.

December 8

"Doctor, doctor, help! I've swallowed some Christmas decorations."
"Yes, I can see you have a touch of tinselitis."

December
9

What do you get if you cross an apple with a Christmas tree?

A pineapple!

December
10

What do you call a chicken at the North Pole?

Lost.

December 11

Why did the gingerbread man go to the doctor?
Because he was feeling crummy!

December 12

What do you get if you cross an Irish setter and a pointer at Christmas-time?
A Pointsetter.

December 13

What happens when Frosty the Snowman gets dandruff?
He gets snowflakes.

December 14

What do reindeer always say before telling you a joke?
"This one will sleigh you!"

December 15

Why did the elf sleep in the fireplace?
He wanted to sleep like a log.

December 16

What's red and white and red and white and red and white?
Santa Claus rolling down a hill.

December 17

How did Rudolf learn to read?
He was elf-taught.

December 18

What do they call a wild elf in Texas?
Gnome on the range!

December 19

What is Santa's favourite breakfast cereal?

Frosted flakes.

December 20

What Christmas carol is popular in the desert?

O camel ye faithful.

December
21

What kind of pine has the sharpest needles?
A porcupine.

December
22

What did the sheep say to the shepherd?
"Season's Bleatings!"

December
23

What do you get if you deep-fry Santa Claus?
Crisp Cringle.

Christmas Eve

Why does Santa go down the chimney on Christmas Eve?

Because it soots him.

Christmas Day

What does Santa get if he's stuck in a chimney?

Claustrophobic!

Where does Santa stay when he's on holiday?

At a ho-ho-hotel!

Where did the mistletoe go to become rich and famous?

Hollywood.

December 28

What does Frosty the Snowman take when he gets sick?
A chill pill.

December 29

What do you get if you cross a skunk with a bell?
Jingle smells.

December 30

Why are Christmas trees like bad knitters?

They both drop their needles!

December 31

New Year's Eve

How do you make an idiot laugh on New Year's Eve?

Tell him a joke on Christmas Day.